THIS BOOK
BELONGS TO

A LITTLE OWL BOOK
BOOK OF PRAYERS

compiled by Hilda Young
illustrated by Annabel Spenceley

WORLD & WHITMAN

Our Father, which art in heaven,
Hallowed be Thy Name.
Thy Kingdom come,
Thy will be done on earth
as it is in heaven.
Give us this day our daily bread.
And forgive us our trespasses,
as we forgive them
that trespass against us.
And lead us not into temptation,
but deliver us from evil:
For thine is the kingdom,
the power and the glory,
for ever and ever.
AMEN

Jesus, friend of little children,
At the start of this new day,
Be thou my guide and helper,
In my work and in my play.

Dear Lord, this new day will come only once.
Before it is gone, help me to do all the good I can,
so that today will not be wasted, and I shall remember
it with happiness.

All good gifts around us
Are sent from heaven above;
O thank the Lord, O thank the Lord,
For all His love.

Be present at our table, Lord;
Be here and everywhere adored.
Thy creatures bless and grant that we
May feast in paradise with Thee.

Make me patient, kind and gentle
Day by day;
Teach me to live more nearly as I pray.

Day by day,
Dear Lord, I pray,
To see Thee more clearly,
To love Thee more dearly,
To follow Thee more nearly,
Day by day.

God bless all those that I love;
God bless all those who love me:
God bless the people of every nation,
At home and beyond the sea.

O fill my heart with quietness,
When I am deep in prayer,
That I may hear you speak to me
And know that you are there.

Lord, make me an instrument of Thy peace;
Where there is hatred, let me sow love;
Where there is injury, pardon;
Where there is discord, union;
Where there is doubt, faith;
Where there is despair, hope;
Where there is darkness, light;
Where there is sadness, joy.

Teach me, my God and King,
In all things Thee to see,
And what I do in anything
To do it as for Thee.

Here a little child I stand,
Heaving up my little hands.
Cold as paddocks* though they be,
Here I lift them up to Thee,
For a benison to fall
On our meat and on us all.

*An old word for toads.

Loving Jesus, gentle lamb,
In Thy gracious hands I am,
Make me, Saviour, what Thou art.
Live Thyself within my heart.

He prayeth best, who loveth best,
All creatures great and small;
For the dear God who loved us,
He made and loveth all.

I see the moon,
And the moon sees me.
God bless the sailors
On the sea.

For the morning sun so bright,
For rest and shelter through the night,
For health and food, for love and friends,
For every gift Thy goodness sends
We thank Thee, gracious Lord.

We thank Thee, heavenly Father,
Who gives us everything,
Who sends the sunshine and showers,
And makes rich harvest spring.
You clothe the lilies of the field,
And feed each bird and beast;
And all may share Thy tender care
The greatest and the least.

For food and all Thy gifts of love,
We give thanks and praise,
Look down, O Father, from above,
And bless us all our days.

Dear Lord Jesus, help me to grow up good and kind, so that my parents will be proud of me. Bless my parents who love and care for me, and help me not to hurt them in any way.

Father, lead me through the day,
Ever in Thy own sweet way;
Teach me to be pure and true,
Show me what I ought to do.

When I'm tempted to do wrong,
Make me steadfast, wise and strong;
And when all alone I stand,
Shield me with Thy mighty hand.

Thank you for the mouse so small,
Thank you for the tree so tall,
Our thanks for all the things that live,
Our thanks for everything you give.

O Lord, bless our school. Let teachers and pupils work together in Thy Name, helping one another, so that our days may be spent wisely and happily, as one big happy family.

Matthew, Mark, Luke and John,
God bless this bed that I lie on.
Four corners to my bed,
Four angels round my head.
One to sing and one to pray,
And two to watch till break of day.